what we have
except when we are lost

By Maria Zajkowski

By MTC Cronin

what we have
except when we are lost

Maria Zajkowski
MTC Cronin

Spuyten Duyvil

New York City

© 2020 M.T.C. Cronin and Maria Zajkowski

ISBN 978-1-949966-79-4

Cover design by Tim Cronin

Library of Congress Cataloging-in-Publication Data

Names: Zajkowski, Maria, author. | Cronin, M. T. C., 1963- author.
Title: What we have : except when we are lost /
Maria Zajkowski, MTC Cronin.
Description: New York City : Spuyten Duyvil, [2020] |
Identifiers: LCCN 2020024327 | ISBN 9781949966794 (paperback)
Subjects: LCGFT: Poetry.
Classification: LCC PR9619.3.Z35 W47 2020 | DDC 821/.914--dc23
LC record available at https://lccn.loc.gov/2020024327

I felt I was walking along a shoreline
of something rather than somewhere.

NATHAN SHEPHERDSON
(ON READING 'WHAT WE HAVE
EXCEPT WHEN WE ARE LOST')

the dream filled with emptiness
spills into the next dream

no eavesdrops on yes
and cannot repeat what it hears

perfectly, says falling,
to free our will from its willingness

last night when you were dead
I hid in the roof and counted my lives

some of them were yours

a window can't be copied
yet after facsimiles exist

my life in comets
heads out of perfection

my body opens yours
I walk into the same wall every day

you left you
the first arrow

repeats

I return to the stars
they are all strangers

all the voices inside
knew you as the outstretched night

explosions die under your wings
I am on my knees in a shrinking room

you don't like it when I crawl
through myself crying

black frost catches all loss in its dark arms

god was never going to be happy in this story
we took his face and buried this field

two horses face backwards
between the owl and the dead owl

ice heads home in the dark
it shuffles the broken leaves at its feet

the horses are examples
of things which do not exist

a horse in my dream is not a horse

even the moon is a secret
a woman walks in the garden that is gone

I write on strips of paper wrapped around rocks
that are buried in the ground

you know how it goes: buried in the ground
is buried in the ground

fight your way out
in other people's sorrow

so much resemblance

does it always dawn slowly?
the butterflies leave my eyes

but death sits in the heart
like death sits unseen in a dark room

the intersection of parallels
a fjord erupting with depth

a new moon arrives with a fortune
and then the light

the light comes true

with the apple in my hand
I will reach you

you will leave my dreams of the high woods
that day after day I sent clouds for

at the mouth of the stone
I hear water turn away

on the edge of grasslands
my soul burns black

the earth recognizes its name

trees rinse their lines in dusk
life drifts towards the present in one long unbroken stream

sounds of a forest cross the distance
a valley in the wind's throat

the lake's warm surface shifts
at the back of my mind

I feel as though I have moved into this house
twenty years after I first lived in it

long ago I remember every day

time calls the veil darling again
what sort of compliment is it

to mislead someone?
in dreams you keep kissing me

I can feel the fish in my DNA
a small wild tree tangled in wire

unsure of what is taken
I wake to another season

unlocking dissolves

when I am dead
I am not forced to explain

how the numbers changed
above my head

your prayer imitates
the blinding of our statues

the eye of the past
rising above the blackened tree

no philosophy in fire

smaller and smaller recalls
the gap through which it came

I saw you lying down with your heart
it wasn't love

I dream of moving
while the root holds the stone

I am where there is just
breath erasing breath

I took off my coat and laid down in my life

all around us mathematics is lying
you count the old game

how long do you think
you can take one day

you keep checking on what is lost
while time flounders to nothing's hum

I am what is left
hands useless as they are in dreams

singing the long stems into the glass

church songs
all the silence in the world is an art

we are fastened in it
we are all speaking

in life above
and the languages nobody spoke

we worked out how to be alive
(sometimes dreams come true)

without you

I think about god
he stood by the fire last night

with his head in the dark
close enough and too far

just like everything to do
lay the table with closed eyes

dream the world on its back
in cries caught underground

I lie to god in my sleep

I was woken
and I was seen

you saw your self
you live on easily outside the body

now we are no longer the smoke in our minds
we exchange flames at the rusty gate

they reveal this fresh, bright judgment
the world is the image of what we have

except when we are lost

we build a boat
to replace where we were going

god escapes from the forest
shuts the river down

our names pass over us
but are not caught

there is a rumour that behind us is nothing
ahead are beginnings

so very temporary

in the past
it's not so complicated to be alone

now when we open our mouths
so many flowers and so much smoke

we say the truth burning but the bees
never buzzed for the sake of a word

the sun you said was not the same
as the one in the sky

human fate isn't human

your body becomes a body
my lies come true

my bed is broken
the last thing comes true

your body is a body
I ask if they can leave you here

they say it is not allowed
I wish you, I close my eyes and wish you

you don't come true

you don't have ears, eyes, fingers
some of the world gets too close

'in some story
there's still a good reason for the world'

talking in my sleep is the same
as any other break in the silence

faith always happens in the dark
you don't wake me

you aren't

once I could move
my hand

it was a sunflower
that turned to the mind

now I have glass arms
stained windows in my wrist

glass has my eyes
they threaten to smash everything

the danger is more than a few lifelines

eight horizons
the torrential voice of the cicadas

your paring knife untouched
in the drawer

peeling oranges with my hands
life burns in the button grass

you slip in and out
of photographs emptying

to look at a wish forbidden

my throat was always full of emptiness
even the moon

I have one in the mirror
I have the effigy of a mirror

whatever makes me
sits with one eye on the sound

trying to catch the moment
a breath stops starting

I have the shot

machines stacked
against clouds

122 chairs
and I know what they're all thinking

the actions of the stars
mimic you dreaming

a hoax travels
a tunnel made from birds

the interference of life is gone

you die in the morning
when the sun has landed

you don't expect light to have sound
someone inserts their body into the garden

my heaven is under your heaven
making a river today

my head closes behind a retrograde
what more do you want when you can't

untouched is not unmade

in arms
I stole from oblivion

things lie rigid
apples are all wood

there is too much colour
the house can't sing

its one floor moves me around my life
sorrow is a single day

inhabited by it we terrify God

the sun is in love with your death
just born

someone must have had the idea of it
closed the world

organized forgetting
for the bits of eternity left over in me

I waste the light
it is supply

I ran out of you

is this memory, this hollow?
you come in

all harbours succeed because of emptiness
you leave a hook in my dream

I can't get you away
land leaves to live on land

exactly like life leaving
I hear you digging

(with) your hand in my heart

we are each other's tombs
you lower me over your eyes

I am being my ending in you
I stop

I do not I am
again and again I just don't know how to

the thing they say doesn't exist does
you go to your head like everything

your gold eyes exact about life leaving

I listen to trees
witnessing the wind

*having gives birth
to what is born of loss*

how might the stars
accept longing as longing

the moon tries again
to catch my moods in the ocean

blue-drenched blade

in your eye a newborn volcano
erupting blindly into ash

the idea of a stone
the yellow silence of the flower

stamens so soft you don't know
if you are touching them

parsing one hand to another
the same becomes unique

I want to pray to a different thing

can you say the world
the word has run out of resources

following you a small black dash
this murderous punctuation

all warfare
the executioners peer through me

'we have ways of making you live'
in language

sometimes these are your words

fate overtaken
by what your beginning crawls back to

your time of birth alters
much more is the same

the lost remind us of themselves
with you never could

harking back ·
or stranded in now

simultaneously nothing

(why are you impossible now?)
I overhear the words that killed you

nothing is as good as the sun, you said,
also slowly dying

the body enters the ruins of life
with one small candle

there is nothing but the secret
that nothing is complete

all of it

the sun and the bird mate for life
harm and the organ of desire

inside the body bodies
a face a fence

I have the apple that grew in my mouth
a mystery for certain

the tension of a lasting calm
(I know fifty-seven)

the alarms of demand and its many farces

I am the arrow
that is your death backwards

already is dead
already

like a breath broken
in the soul's throat

the last myth told me
to put a wreath on your head

hands full of poems full of thorns

the fence that doesn't exist
separates what is from what is

the secret dangles
from the unimagined mouth

find a path
that breaks with the body

through you the world struggles
to get to the next place

next can't

if I begin
we both break with confidence

a wind that blows so fast
nothing moves

'you can't leave' a leaf
says on the way down

the moon grazes my head
with the opening phrase:

why share this thing that nobody owns

the sky in the road kept blowing away
the road that kept us in this place

half of your death lies down
no dishonest clutter

I could hear it in my hands
closer inside

we hope the top of the world is still
but your face falls down

doesn't exist

I wave at you
but you are in love again

the thing you pay to be told
you know more than the money

crime of total knowing
but you didn't hear backwards

didn't see backwards
didn't know that life

isn't this one

you stop
I stop

and the hand stops
next to my heart

a hand folds me
into another hand

I am sure I am something in flight
trying to fight my way out

of time's scaffolding

you sleep for everyone
withholding sorrows

in your eyes lives something
that cannot see

a small eternity fastens you
to the time on the clock

when I undo all the screws
the world falls back together

love bolted down!

I have bruises from where I escaped
from language

my body is ready
to have no name

my teeth move
into the sound of my voice

say slavery
completing myself immediately

catastrophe of joy

the moon upside down
among the other superstitions

I meet you in the ash
I read your face aloud

the zero point
you say it's just a chariot

leaving our intentions
all the nowheres

I drop fires on the killing planet

sitting in the steel nail's soul
I see chemistry growing cold

logic has erected
a gallows in my chest

there is a single tongue
cutting a mountain in half

monotonous afternoon of earth
chases me into your dark arms

where life gapes

the photo fallen
behind the kitchen bench

tears at my future and throws
down whistling seconds

a bomb going off in *I remember
you driving home*

*with the cat
on your shoulder* you

cannot enter or leave a memory

the world is taking itself back
daffodil by daffodil

my actual lives
life by life

numbers slip into my blood
and count the days

a golden string measures
the precision of your absence

in it you come before and after nothing

the soft plug of words
is pulled from my throat

leaves only the guttural
mouth-to-mouth tenancy

'we are the same'
then I saw you

shattered hunting
remnant of the hunt

I haven't told anyone who you are

door of the corpse
opens and the electric stops me

like a glamour gag
that I cannot bear how this

could have not been this
climbing up the synapse

everyone guards their own grave
unnecessarily

it cannot be taken

a promise ascends from your feet
unacceptable joy

reaching out for hermits
or indivine comets

the night-sign of an echo
a mountain hatches a moon

buries my room in the woods
above wolf stars

a passage to the seen

on the map your back is breaking mine
if I was on the page

the page would ignore me
turn of your head away

towards the whole lot that is done
gesture of a million traces

closing atlas of the paths of you –
there are dead ends

in all of us

the bird who forgot
the pilgrimage to a beginning

the flower's answer dispersed
on a ruined sea of earth

you escaped through the map
throwing a net around the dream

the void of dawn
opening the moth

from which all light comes

to do:
get closer to the colour of your eyes

sand and rock changing places
in and out of the river

more of the vision
most perfectly water's shadow

surface that reflects me
beyond evolution

these variations on elegance

I have been
once again your litany

for the fire above us
elevation by changing your name

A Title for the Living
all existence enters your fingertips

I am your volunteer
so are you

my choice is that I had none

I carry you in my mouth for protection
what more can the dead ask

ignorant glistening tongue
full of quotes

whips/
husk

from this prison I compose
sentences of the heart

at night I count words not sheep

I have dreamed you
lining up dreams to make a life

tying the days together
evening failed in dawn

you always said there is an ideal goat
to eat away at the join

even so this knot never unravels
in its bind I see you

coming back to death

until the idea can meet the idea
all words are the same word

galvanic uselessness
meaning knitted to its undoing

inexact is the tool
that can be put to any use

your bottom line
was that sometimes in a paddock

you didn't want to be a horse

every flower
escapes our nightmares

left there as your debt
the key is a sign of destitution

black plumage
the winter of your face

when I wake they say
wow, gorgeous, did you fuck?

I don't remember to want anyone

little dust-coloured bird
that clings to the music

sound of the scaffold
which has finally found weight

in the secret's own branches
mutilated and real

dust expressing your body
repositioned in the world

small foot in the forked snow

the blurred wolf guards
its own subtle loss

iris flooded
with envy and idleness

you don't act like my lover
your bridge your bride

you cross it carrying a saucepan
shouting my credentials

no beginning ending like the last

a dog smells it in a photograph
the grass shedding you

crater of the sky formed
by the first ball thrown

trees growing
toward the earth beyond

they grieve incandescence
put down their roots

in a mirage

a tree opens high among the other souls
a catapulted moon breaks at my feet

like the hawk, (*detail*), & hour after
it's all a miracle before it is

I was observing you refrain
the world that didn't have you in it

times and places
to be exact is specifically impossible

when I pick a flower I die

taking the small green pill
seeing with the green pill's eyes

silent luminous food
snakelings on a bed of cellophane

a giant bird eating the books
of your body and voice

hallucinations have your name
(but I know what the cloud said

about all those images)

this mute thick crawling
through the gasp of one flower

singing the unstoppable grief of horses
pressing against the thinness of the chest wall

you'd think god was busy
with his lips on the cure

(say yes) to what burned say yes
the sky that took my hand last night

as though I was ready

I saw them breaking the angel apart
every piece had its own heart

absolute vision
which closed me

inside these birds
a reverence translated

the lie which wasn't before it was told
(if we are honest)

redefining grace

a world without flags
where souls are the flags

infinite infinite luck
you can die of

when I'm here I live here
houses no houses

release the mountain
by placing your foot

chaos has now

everyone in the world
is solving for 'x'

– sentinel of nothing
– luxury of regret

while the accident slips in unseen
radioactive pears on the pear tree

a crow plays my name
'blue swans in the valley'

I sit in an archway with sobs in its arch

listening at the ripe wall
cuntroom talk

someone turns a key in the wolf
and unlocks all nights at once

the shape of a dark room
nothing but a shape

imagine having you
imagine having you!

I go to sleep inside a lie

take a measurement of the end
they have even lost the knife

that cut you away
the way you fell from everything

was like a play with one aside
lines delivered

in the pure divide of empty time:
'how can I be sure

I am being properly betrayed?'

I stood face first in the box
around now insert theories

the house that stands in my mind is inside-out
each room is young

my breakfast is sour
I spoon my reflection over the walls

at the end of the sky
a scavenger very quietly fills you with views

this day from here

eternity falls from view
down the curve of your skull

the presence of absence
what is never enough is enough

why do I need to live anywhere
every day the house moves to another street

in the glass of 24 hours
I'll have you back

by this I am reminded

the season anticipates other seasons
orders the darkness

I hang from my foot
between two earths

all the space let go into space
the hand that comes back

I place my head in the lake
there is room for one night

one night is all it takes

that the touch ten times sugar
remembers amnesia

your prohibited living
how did you sell me this

flat on the floor the ground
practising you for years

I might lie here until the wood rots
feel of one toe against another

all I feel

dead, you disbelieve me
nothing matters as much

I stay with what cannot touch me
………………………………..

fucking is religion
making a song of the world's chaos

undoing longing
I died in my body

putting your existence to my lips

just when you would ask
I had it all

beneath my name
is everything unread

entered by love rape dusty sand
one thousand libraries where they file

without stakes
here your death writes in rejoinder

each weeping point of the universe

should I keep writing
or look for you?

(you stay at the electric fence
your whole life)

shouting making
to get it done

lift to get it lifted and kill to get it killed
this is a world

where I can't decide what happens

everyone walked like you
every day of the year wears a black hood

the whole world
has gone somewhere else

I am every refugee
and the host

my heart keeping the beat
devotion

blow by dying blow

belief understands
I look ahead

the rows of the dead
punching down the punch lines

between tremors
as close to breath as I can edge

a silver line has all along been
freeing my argument from yours

the moon a body is not

I know you're not lost
but where are you?

you are not in any language
the same in any language

your existence haunts better
than this

white tattoo
on a white page

invisible sail of memory

warm death around my neck
I am already cold

otherless
we all have two meanings

even a stone
tousles with mystery

your language
translates into your language

ungrateful to be grateful

the different consistent call
is always of opposites

no-one's name is their name
when they do not hear it

not what I want to say
but what I hear

whispering into loudspeakers
what is taken

hides our hearts

MTC Cronin has published over twenty
books of poetry and essays.

Maria Zajkowski is a poet and librettist based in Melbourne, Australia.

www.ingramcontent.com/pod-product-compliance
Lightning Source LLC
Chambersburg PA
CBHW010346170726
48284CB00009B/2803